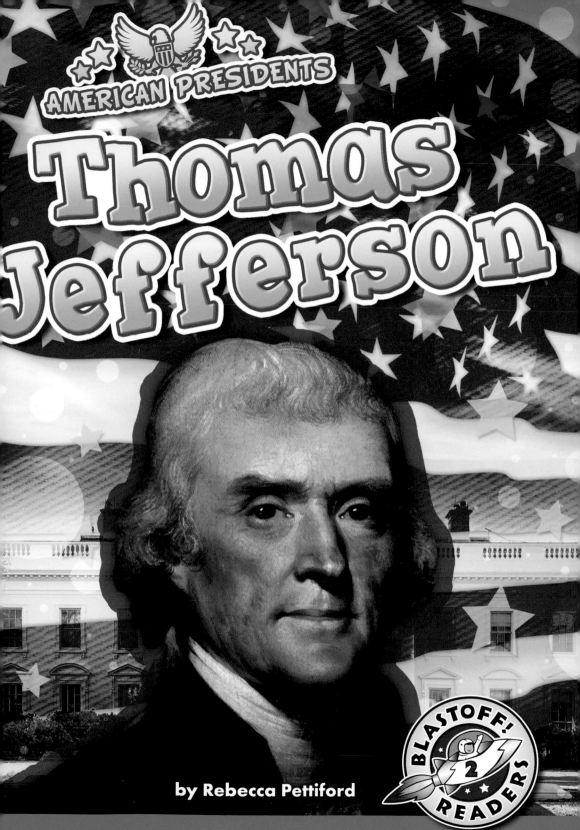

AMERICAN PRESIDENTS

Thomas Jefferson

by Rebecca Pettiford

BLASTOFF! READERS
2

BELLWETHER MEDIA · MINNEAPOLIS, MN

Blastoff! Readers are carefully developed by literacy experts to build reading stamina and move students toward fluency by combining standards-based content with developmentally appropriate text.

Level 1 provides the most support through repetition of high-frequency words, light text, predictable sentence patterns, and strong visual support.

Level 2 offers early readers a bit more challenge through varied sentences, increased text load, and text-supportive special features.

Level 3 advances early-fluent readers toward fluency through increased text load, less reliance on photos, advancing concepts, longer sentences, and more complex special features.

★ **Blastoff! Universe**

Reading Level

Grade **K**

Grades **1-3**

DISCOVERY

Grade **4**

This edition first published in 2022 by Bellwether Media, Inc.

No part of this publication may be reproduced in whole or in part without written permission of the publisher. For information regarding permission, write to Bellwether Media, Inc., Attention: Permissions Department, 6012 Blue Circle Drive, Minnetonka, MN 55343.

Library of Congress Cataloging-in-Publication Data

Names: Pettiford, Rebecca, author.
Title: Thomas Jefferson / by Rebecca Pettiford.
Description: Minneapolis, MN : Bellwether Media, Inc., 2022. | Series: Blastoff! readers: American presidents | Includes bibliographical references and index. | Audience: Ages 5-8 | Audience: Grades 2-3 | Summary: "Relevant images match informative text in this introduction to Thomas Jefferson. Intended for students in kindergarten through third grade"-- Provided by publisher.
Identifiers: LCCN 2021011417 (print) | LCCN 2021011418 (ebook) | ISBN 9781644875193 (library binding) | ISBN 9781648344879 (paperback) | ISBN 9781648344275 (ebook)
Subjects: LCSH: Jefferson, Thomas, 1743-1826--Juvenile literature. | Presidents--United States--Biography--Juvenile literature.
Classification: LCC E332.79 .P465 2022 (print) | LCC E332.79 (ebook) | DDC 973.4/6092 [B]--dc23
LC record available at https://lccn.loc.gov/2021011417
LC ebook record available at https://lccn.loc.gov/2021011418

Editor: Elizabeth Neuenfeldt   Designer: Josh Brink

Printed in the United States of America, North Mankato, MN.

Table of Contents

Who Was Thomas Jefferson?

Thomas Jefferson was the third president of the United States. He served from 1801 to 1809.

He made the U.S. bigger.

THOMAS JEFFERSON
THE FATHER
OF
EXPANSION

Thomas's Hometown

Shadwell,
Virginia

Thomas was born in 1743. He was raised in Shadwell, Virginia.

He had nine brothers and sisters.

Thomas's childhood home

Thomas loved to learn.
He studied many subjects
in college.

Presidential Picks

Foods

vanilla ice cream and
macaroni and cheese

Hobbies

reading, writing letters,
and playing violin

Games

chess and
backgammon

Animals

mockingbirds, dogs,
and grizzly bears

Later, he worked in the
Virginia government.

During the **Revolutionary War**, Thomas wrote the **Declaration of Independence**. He wanted **freedom** from British rule.

After the war, he was a **diplomat**. He later became the vice president!

Thomas writing the Declaration of Independence

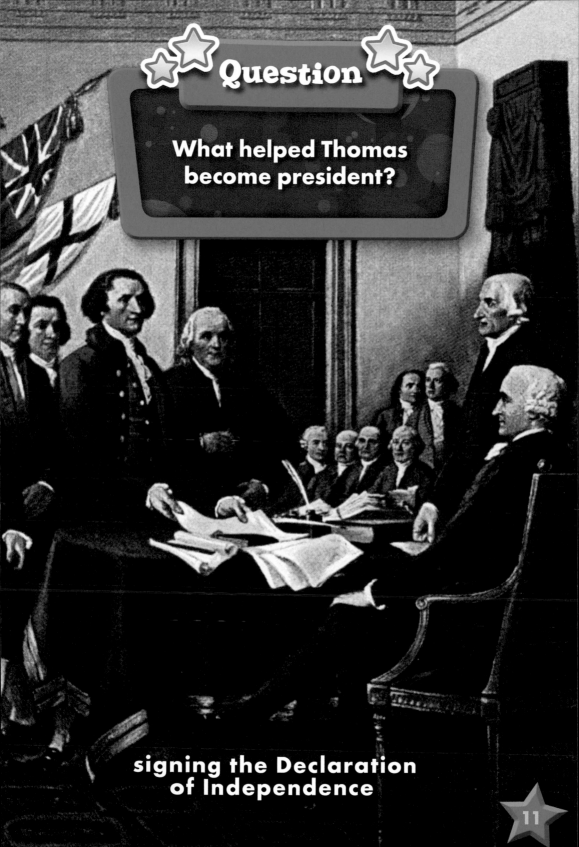

What helped Thomas become president?

signing the Declaration of Independence

Thomas was **elected** president on February 17, 1801. The election was close!

His **term** began on March 4.

Presidential Profile

Place of Birth

Shadwell, Virginia

Birthday

April 13, 1743

Schooling

College of William and Mary

Term

1801 to 1809

Party

Democratic-Republican

Signature

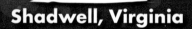

Vice Presidents

Aaron Burr

George Clinton

13

War began with **Tripoli** in May.
Pirates took U.S. sailors as the
war carried on.

Thomas made the U.S. **Navy** stronger. He helped the U.S. win!

In 1803, Thomas made the **Louisiana Purchase**. It doubled the size of the U.S.

It helped Thomas get reelected in 1804. He won by many votes!

celebrating the
Louisiana Purchase

France and Britain
at war

At this time, France and Britain were at war. The war created problems for U.S. trade. Thomas signed the **Embargo Act**. It stopped U.S. trade with other countries.

Thomas Timeline

March 4, 1801

Thomas Jefferson begins his term

February 6, 1802

The war against Tripoli begins

April 30, 1803

Thomas makes the Louisiana Purchase

December 5, 1804

Thomas is reelected

June 4, 1805

Thomas ends the war with Tripoli

December 22, 1807

Thomas signs the Embargo Act

March 4, 1809

Thomas leaves office

19

What Thomas Left Behind

Thomas left office in 1809. He died on July 4, 1826.

He helped the U.S. become what it is today!

THOMAS JEFFERSON
1743–1826

Glossary

Declaration of Independence—a document that was signed on July 4, 1776, that stated the 13 American colonies were free from British rule

diplomat—a person who works to make sure countries get along

elected—chosen by voting

Embargo Act—a law passed in 1807 that stopped the U.S. from trading with other countries; an embargo is a government order that stops or limits trade with other countries.

freedom—the state of being free

Louisiana Purchase—a deal made between France and the United States; it gave the United States 828,000 square miles (2,144,510 square kilometers) of land west of the Mississippi River.

navy—the part of a country's military that fights at sea

pirates—people that attack and steal from ships at sea

Revolutionary War—the war from 1775 to 1783 in which the United States fought for independence from Britain

term—the length of time in which a person holds office or a position

Tripoli—a city in North Africa

To Learn More

AT THE LIBRARY

Forest, Christopher. *Louisiana Purchase*. Minneapolis, Minn.: Pogo Books, 2021.

Murray, Laura K. *Thomas Jefferson*. Minneapolis, Minn.: Capstone, 2020.

Ransom, Candice. *Thomas Jefferson*. Minneapolis, Minn.: Pop!, 2019.

ON THE WEB

FACTSURFER

Factsurfer.com gives you a safe, fun way to find more information.

1. Go to www.factsurfer.com.

2. Enter "Thomas Jefferson" into the search box and click 🔍.

3. Select your book cover to see a list of related content.

Index